MW00721101

# A Short Review of Dr. Jung's Article
# Redemption Ideas In Alchemy

*By* M. Esther Harding, M.D.

## <u>Printing Statement:</u>

Due to the very old age and scarcity of this book, many of the pages may be hard to read due to the blurring of the original text, possible missing pages, missing text and other issues beyond our control.

Because this is such an important and rare work, we believe it is best to reproduce this book regardless of its original condition.

Thank you for your understanding.

# A Short Review of Dr. Jung's Article

# Redemption Ideas In Alchemy

## BEING A LECTURE DELIVERED BEFORE THE ANALYTICAL PSYCHOLOGY CLUB OF NEW YORK CITY, OCTOBER, 1937

### By M. ESTHER HARDING, M.D.

The article which I am going to review was sent to the Club by Dr. Jung himself. It is a reprint from the Eranos Yarbuch of 1936 and consists of the text of two lectures which Dr. Jung gave before the pyschological conference in Ascona. The original is in German and up to date there has been no official translation. Dr. Kristine Mann, however, undertook to translate it for us and my knowledge of the article is based on her preliminary work, for which we all have to thank her.

The article itself is exceedingly erudite, being copiously annotated with source material, partly in Latin, and drawing upon ancient and mediaeval philosophical material little known to the average educated person. Dr. Jung assumes that his hearers will be familiar with historical personages and their work and will understand allusions to classics, both philosophical and religious, to which I must admit I was in great part a stranger before I hunted up a few of the more important references, and even now my knowledge of these old thinkers and their writings is practically limited to a few quotations.

This being the case it seemed to me wiser not to attempt to read you the whole of the article, and indeed it is far too long for one evening's talk, but rather to tell you as simply as I can what are the main themes which Dr. Jung elaborates in so masterly a fashion. With the exception of the introduction I shall use Dr. Jung's actual words and merely link the quoted passages together with connecting phrases and explanations.

[ 1 ]

First of all, there is a point that I want to call to your attention though Dr. Jung himself does not make it except by implication, and that is the contribution which he himself makes to the subject. The meaning and significance of alchemy was entirely obscure until he threw a beam of light upon it from his profound understanding. Having read his article one says, "How stupid the other commentators were not to have seen at once what the alchemists were after," and one tends to forget that this is exactly what one feels inclined to say about any obscure subject towards which Jung turns his attention.

The modern commentators on alchemy, excluding Jung, fall into two groups. The first, the chemical-minded, see in alchemy only the forerunner of chemistry. They interpret the enthusiasm and devotion of the alchemists, many of whom spent years of their lives and all of their fortunes on the work, as due to a hope of finding material gold and so of making themselves masters of this world's wealth. Undoubtedly many so-called alchemists were moved by such motives and there exist countless treatises which are concerned with the making of gold, or the tingeing of the base metals so that they would simulate gold. Indeed some authorities believe that alchemy originated in Egypt as a by-product of the embalmers' art, which needed large quantities of gold paint for the sarcophagi. It has even been suggested that the word alchemy is derived from Chem, the old name of Egypt. But it is more probable that it has to do with Chem, black, for the black substance, as we shall see later, played a large part in alchemical processes. In their own day these gold makers, or would-be gold makers, were called "puffers," not with the modern slang connotation of self-advertisers, but probably because they worked with blast furnaces. Among the puffers were many honest metallurgists and also many dishonest charlatans, who sought only to profit by deceiving the credulous.

In addition to these puffers were others who even in their own day were called "true alchemists." It is in regard to this group that opinion has been so sharply divided. Commentators, such as the French chemist, Berthelot, who translated, or caused to be translated, all the main Greek, Syriac, and Arabian texts, treat the material as if it were intended to be chemical research, which somehow became contaminated with superstitious aims and beliefs, much as a metal in its natural state as ore is mixed and obscured by dross; and furthermore that the truth, that is, the chemical truth, was intentionally concealed under the most fantastic analogies and allegorical stories.

The very same treatises have been reviewed, however, by another group

[ 2 ]

of commentators who interpret them in an entirely different way. In their opinion the alchemists were really teaching a mystical philosophy which had nothing to do with chemistry. The chemical form of the texts, as well as the actual retorts and furnaces of the alchemical workers, were in their opinion a blind, a disguise, consciously adopted by the adepts in order to conceal their real meaning from the vulgar. Perhaps the most important exponent of this view is Mrs. Atwood, who wrote a mystical and theosophical treatise on the subject in the seventies of the last century.

Certain other writers, such as Edward Arthur Waite, who translated many of the Latin texts into English, and John Read, professor of Chemistry at St. Andrews University, Scotland, and whose book, *Prelude to Chemistry*, makes perhaps the best introduction to the subject, take an intermediate position, recognizing that in many of the texts chemistry and philosophy are inextricably mixed. But neither of them understand why this should be so; they can explain it only as due to the inferior thinking of those ancient days.

In his most suggestive book, *Problems of Mysticism and Its Symbolism*, Herbert Silberer, a Freudian analyst, attempted to synthesize these opposing points of view. He took certain alchemistic parables and other writings, all of late date, and interpreted them analytically. His explanation hovers around the "secret," so that one thinks every minute he is going to unravel it, but he never solves the enigma. Indeed, one even comes to doubt whether he really saw the problem at all. He comes up to it and slides away from it, leaving us with a rather unsatisfactory ethical or mystical explanation very remote from Jung's scientific and logical discussion.

When Jung takes hold of the enigma he shows at once that the admixture of chemistry and philosophy was not fortuitous but inevitable. He begins his lecture by pointing out that in the early centuries alchemy was concerned with the secret of matter, the material substance of which the world is made, and which was at that time *the* great unknown. Rocks and soils occurring in the natural state were taken for granted by the average person, who never questioned what they were made of nor speculated about the strange unknown properties which their constituents might possess if only they could be separated from their mutual bondage to each other. Chemical substances which to-day form the most ordinary equipment of every household and every factory were formerly completely unknown. For it was not until the eighteenth century that the growing science of chemistry began to throw light on the nature of matter and of chemical processes. The alchemists deserve the name of great thinkers if only because they could ask a question about that self-evident and taken-for-granted "matter," whose answer, still uncompleted, is the objective of many of our modern sciences.

"Prior to the seventeenth century," says Dr. Jung, "when many alchemists abandoned their retorts and fusing cauldrons and gave themselves up to philosophical speculations, alchemists were concerned with the dark and unknown secrets of matter, which they sought to penetrate by seeking laws and forms in the dark room of the unconscious. What the alchemist saw and thought that he recognized were in fact his own unconscious contents. For the unconscious contents were projected, as they always are, into that secret unknown matter which fascinates and attracts the searcher after truth."

For the seekers of many centuries this "matter" was the actual concrete material substance of the world. For us this is now for the most part no longer mysterious, but is the subject of the natural sciences, chemistry, physics, and so on. Yet perhaps in new physics we shall have to recognize again a projection field of the unconscious, but that problem is for most of us a side issue. For *us* the realm into which the unconscious projection flows unchecked is more nearly psychic; it is, namely, the substance of life itself; situations, circumstances, and relationships, personal, national, even international. Here is to be found the material for a modern alchemy. And strangely enough the laws and forms which the old alchemists describe as relating to matter seem to hold true of these more modern enigmas too, if we are to rely on the evidence obtained from the analytic procedure.

Dr. Jung begins the subject matter of his lecture with a brief summary of the main processes the alchemists employed in the search for the final product, which is sometimes spoken of as gold, sometimes as the stone of the philosophers, and sometimes as the elixir of life. The description of these processes varies considerably from one text to another, but the following is a generally valid outline.

The process begins with a *prima materia,* or first material, whose nature is one of the great mysteries of alchemy and in the search for which many years of the alchemist's life were usually expended. This *prima materia* starts in a black condition, called *nigredo.* It is the famous black substance of which so much is heard, not only in alchemy but also in the analytic hour! The next step concerned a union, or *conjunctio,* of a pair of opposites, usually thought of as male and female, which was often represented as a marriage. Immediately there followed a death, dispersion, or *morti-*

*ficatio*, then a washing, *ablutio*, which made the substance white, *albedo*. This white substance was the first result. It was spoken of as the white stone or the white rose.

The next stage was the reddening, or *rubido*, which produced the second result, the red stone or the red rose. As red stone or carbuncle it was also the red tincture or elixir. In the earlier systems this was the end of the process but in some it was followed by a yellowing, *citrinitas*, which produced the coagulated gold, the final result, which was occasionally called *aurum potabile*. This was also the sought-for *lapis philosophorum*, the stone of the philosophers which had the power of changing base metals into gold, and of healing the sick and producing eternal life.

So we see that the stone, the *lapis*, as red tincture is instrumental in the work, but it is also spoken of as the absolute aim of the whole proceeding, when it is a mystic being, having body, soul, and spirit. Indeed the *prima materia* is itself a sort of pre-stage of the *lapis*, and furthermore some texts say that the stone, as the gift of God, must be added to the materials at the very beginning of the operation in order to make the stone, or the gold must be added in order to make the gold!

Next in importance to the *prima materia*, or in some texts even identical with it, is the permanent water, the *aqua permanens*, or hylic water, which is mercury or quicksilver. It plays its mysterious rôle throughout the entire work, and is instrumental in producing the gold. The *vas Hermetis*, the retort or alembic, is also essential; it is the special vessel in which the transformation took place. It, too, is instrumental in the work, for it has unique relations both to the *prima materia* and to the *lapis*. The procedure always took place in a cyclic way, the various steps of the process being repeated many times, so that it was called *circulatio*, or *rotar*, wheel.

The problem of what was the compelling motive that induced the alchemists to labour on and on, spending time and fortune on a work that produced so little chemical result is closely bound up with the problem of their secret. Both these questions are answered by Jung's explanation that the unconscious content of the workers themselves was perceived in the dark and unknown substance of matter. The mysteries of chemical substances and their behaviour represented to the alchemist the secrets of the unknown parts of his own psyche. In the chemical language employed by the alchemists some sort of psychological process was expressed. The alchemists themselves knew that what they carried on was not just ordinary chemistry. For instance, as early as the first century A.D. a tract of Democritus was entitled: "The Physical and the Philosophical." For them the two streams of spiritual and physical flowed together, but we cannot even think of these two things in the same terms. They said, *"tam ethice quam physice"* (as is the spiritual so is the physical); this was axiomatic for them, but it is not clear to our logic.

And so when the alchemist says that he conceals his meaning and the nature of his *prima materia* to prevent the worldly from exploiting his secret by making gold to obtain worldly power, it is largely a rationalization; for the same author will maintain that he is not talking of ordinary gold, the gold of the vulgar, but of "our gold" or "philosophical gold," and indeed that he would speak more clearly if he could. He may perhaps have concealed something which he could have revealed in some cases, but the claim to be able to do so was really not true; for the truth was that he did not know the secret himself. For the real secret is not something known and consciously concealed; the real secret is an unknown fact, which is only dimly discerned through intimations. To the alchemist matter was this unknown fact which contained the secret and, in order to clarify it, he projected his unconscious contents into it, but he did not do this consciously because of a theory, it just happened. He experienced the presence of the idea, the psychic content or archetype, in the physical materials which attracted his attention. So during his experiments the worker had certain psychic experiences which are recorded more or less clearly, especially by the later workers.

These experiences must necessarily have come from the non-personal part of the psyche, and Jung directed his attention to trying to discover whether the alchemists in their accounts of the way in which the materials behaved in their retorts were not really reporting experiences of the non-personal psyche. When he started his research, he was not very sanguine of results for the very fact that these experiences would be of the deeper layers of the unconscious meant that the reports of the workers would be confused for they were reporting something that was inaccessible to them.

He found, however, especially in the more recent tracts, evidence that the workers had visions during the course of their work. In a tract of 1732 there is a report about visions of the creation. "Rain water has to be taken and treated in a certain way, then to be placed in a spherical goblet which has been cut in half. Then a drop of consecrated wine must be dropped in and a vision of the primal darkness above the waters will be seen. A second drop is added and light will be seen penetrating the darkness as at the Creation. Further drops up to six are added and the six steps of the Creation are spread before the eyes." Directions for many similar

[ 6 ]

experiments are to be found in the texts. In a tract of the sixteenth century Theobald de Hoghelands says that the visions seen in the work are like the figures imagined in the fire or in the clouds.

The alchemists even made a further step in what appears to be psychological understanding of what they were doing when they insisted that what went on in the retort went on also in the worker. In 1500 Trithemius, the teacher of Paracelsus, said in a tract published in the *Theatrum Chemicum*: "You will never make the one out of others, if the one is not first made out of yourself," and in the *Rosarium Philosophorum, 1550,* it is said: "Who also knows the salt and its solution, knows the hidden secret of the old wise men. Direct your mind, therefore, to the salt for in it alone is to be found the science and the most renowned and mysterious secret of all the old philosophers." Jung points out that in Latin the word for *it* is feminine *eam* and refers to the mind not to the salt and that what the text really says is, "Direct your mind to the salt, for in your mind alone is to be found . . . " Salt stood for body, as mercury for spirit, and sulphur for soul, so it would mean direct your spirit to the body or bodily manifestation (that is the symbol) for in your mind alone is to be found the secret.

In another place the anonymous author of the *Rosarium* says that the work must be "done with true imagination and not with fantastic imagination," and another time that the stone will be found "when the work oppresses the worker." This last remark can only be understood as meaning that the psychological attitude of the worker is an indispensible condition for the finding of the wonder stone. And both suggest that the author is of the opinion that the true secret of the art is hidden in the human mind, or expressed in modern terms, that it is in the unconscious. But we have to remember that the understanding of those days was different from ours, for the alchemists considered the psychological changes to be dependent in what we should consider a magical way on the physical changes in the retort. *"Tam ethice quam physice"* implies a sort of *participation mystique* which dealt with the projected unconscious content as if it were actually identical with or inherent in the physical material whose transformation the workers in the alchemical laboratory sought to bring about.

Dr. Jung continues: It is not surprising therefore to find that the alchemists laid great stress on the moral qualities and disposition of the workers, who were also informed that the result was invariably a gift of God and that they must therefore fear God and seek His aid at every step of the work.

The instruction of Morienus to King Calid, reported in a tract of the eighth century, is particularly to the point: "This matter," he wrote, "cannot be won or carried through by means of passion or power. It is won only through patience and humility, and through a resolute and perfect love. God bestows this divine and pure knowledge upon His believers and servants whom He has chosen from the beginning of time to receive them." He later explains that he lives in the wilderness instead of in a cloister "because no one reaps who does not sow . . . above all narrow is the way to peace and no one can travel on it except through the suffering of the soul."

In 1618 Michael Majer says: "There is in chemistry a certain noble body (*lapis*) at whose beginning misery rules with vinegar, but at whose conclusion delight with joyousness; I have therefore assumed that it would happen so" with me too.

Now the difficulty and painfulness of the work is due we are told to the *nigredo*, the black condition of the substance, and also to the "ghastly darkness of our souls." And for its cure Michael Majer says that earnest concentration, *meditatio*, should be practiced with perfect love. And so we come to the extraordinary way in which the alchemists use the terms *meditatio* and *imaginatio*, the second method advised for working on the substance.

The seventeenth century alchemical dictionary of Ruland defines *meditatio* as "holding an inner conversation with an unseen interlocutor or, when one is called, with God or oneself or one's good angel." So *meditatio* signifies making a relation to the answering voice within, that is, to the unconscious.

*Imaginatio*, imagination, is also used in a particular way. During the course of their experiments the alchemists had visions which they tell us were produced by the use of true imagination, as distinguished from fantastic imagination. When we read the alchemical descriptions of *imaginatio*, Jung points out, we have to discard those insubstantial schemes which we gladly represent to ourselves as phantasy pictures, and think of the phantasy process as something substantial, having a body, a very subtle body of half-spiritual nature. For Ruland's dictionary defines *imaginatio* as "the constellation (star) in humanity of the heavenly or superheavenly body."

In an age when there was as yet no psychology of the empirical soul such concretism was necessarily important. For everything unconscious was projected into matter insofar as it was activated, and met man from the outside. The superheavenly or subtle body of which Ruland speaks was both spirit and matter, it was as if it were a spiritual-physical hermaphrodite. And the *imaginatio* is a physico-spiritual activity which can be introduced into the cycle of material changes, affecting them and being affected by them.

Imagination is a concentrated extract of the life powers of the body as well as of the soul, which accounts for the requirement that the alchemist must be of sound physical constitution, for he worked with and through his own quintessence. He was his own indispensable experimental condition. Because of the admixture of the physical and psychical, it always remains obscure whether the results are to be sought in the material or in the spiritual field. But this antithesis is false, for in alchemical thought there was a middle kingdom, between matter and spirit, namely, a soul kingdom of the subtle body, whose appearance was suited to the spiritual as well as to the material.

This in-between kingdom disappears when one examines matter in and for itself, as our modern science does. Also it remains non-existent so long as one thinks one knows something final about the soul and about matter. But in the moment when physical touches upon the unknowable and psychology is forced to recognize that there are contents beyond personally gained consciousness, the in-between kingdom is animated anew and the physical and psychological are again mixed.

Such considerations, says Jung, are unavoidable if one desires to understand the unique terminology of alchemy. Very modern problems are found in alchemy which, however, are not in the realm of chemistry.

Thus the concept of *imaginatio* is one of the most important keys to the understanding of the alchemical work. The anonymous author of the *Tract on Sulphur* gives a clear hint as to the secret of the imaginative capacities of the soul. "The soul," he says, "stands in the place of God, His vice-regent. It dwells in the living spirit, in the pure blood. It rules consciousness which rules the body. The soul thus functions in the body, but carries out the greater part of her functioning outside of the body [which, Jung adds, is in the projection]. This characteristic is divine, for divine wisdom is only in part shut up in the body of the world, in the greater part it is outside and able to imagine many higher things which the body of the world is not able to comprehend. These are outside of nature, God's secrets. The soul, just like God, also imagines many deepest things, outside the body. The soul has absolute power to make things other than the body can comprehend. But it also has the greatest power over the body. So," our author adds, "you can comprehend greater things as we have opened the door for you."

Dr. Jung continues, the soul is obviously an *anima corporalis* which dwells in the blood, that is, in the unconscious. It is below the diaphragm, yet it is also the vice-regent from God. The unconscious is not only a super-consciousness but also an infra-consciousness. This is difficult for us to accept. But the problem does not concern the alchemical philosophers, for according to them every elemental form contains its opposite. So an *anima corporalis* is at the same time spiritual. "The soul," says the author of the *Tract on Sulphur*, "is only in part adherent to the body, just as God is only in part enclosed in the body of the world." That is, the soul is only in part identical with our conscious being, for the rest it is found in the projected condition and there imagines what the body cannot comprehend or bring into being. The alchemists' work corresponded to this activity of the soul outside the body. They say that as the soul has the greatest power over the body, and the art permits you to conceive of the greater, "therefore it can affect your body, with the help of the art and *Deo concedente*, if God permits it."

Thus the *imaginatio* is a making real of those contents of the unconscious which are *extra-naturam*, that is, not given by our empirical world, and are of an *a priori* archetypal nature. The place and the medium of making real are neither matter nor spirit, but in that in-between kingdom, which can be expressed adequately only through the symbol. The symbol is neither abstract nor concrete; neither rational nor irrational; neither real nor unreal; it is indeed both — it is *non vulgi*, the aristrocratic affair of a person set apart, or one chosen by God from the ancient beginnings.

The fundamental concept of alchemy is the *opus*, the work, consisting first of a practical and then a theoretic part. The practical part was concerned with manipulations of metals, particularly quicksilver, but also with sulphur, salts, and so forth. This is complicated and obscure and it is impossible to follow it or to imagine how it was worked, with what kind of matter and with what results. The alchemists themselves were aware of their obscurity. They claimed that they concealed things intentionally but nowhere is it stated that they could be clearer if they would. The fact of the matter is that the darkness which the chemical procedure covers depends on the fact that the alchemist had little concern or interest in the chemical part, but only used it as a nomenclature for the fascinating soul happenings and transmutations which, however, he perceived not in his mind but in the chemical substances in his retort.

[ 10 ]

The second part of the work was called by the alchemists *theoria*, or *amplificatio*, and it was a method of amplification such as we use in interpreting dreams. This theory is the so-called Hermetic philosophy which was greatly broadened in the period just preceding the Reformation, by the assimilation of Christian dogmatic ideas.

These two parts of the alchemical work, the practical and theoretical, are clearly shown in the title vignette of the *Tripus Aureus*, the *Golden Tripod*, of 1677. Here is shown on one side a laboratory with its apparatus and worker while on the other side are the philosophers with their books. In the centre is a tripod with the vase of Hermes containing a winged dragon.

The dragon, says Jung, symbolises the experience, the vision of the alchemist who is both practicing and theorizing. It is a *monstrum*, that is, a symbol, composed of the chthonic principle of the snake, and the air principle of the bird. The dragon is also Mercury, the divine winged Hermes manifesting in heavy material. I will quote what Jung says about this: "The heavy metal of the *argentum vivum*, quicksilver, was the wonderful material which expressed the being of the 'glistening one' and of the living one, who is perfect within. The alchemist speaks of Mercurius, by this he means, exoterically, quicksilver, esoterically, however, he means the divine world-creating spirit concealed in matter. The dragon is indeed the oldest picture-symbol of alchemy. It appears as the *ouroborus*, the tail-eater, in the codex *Marcianus*, which belongs to the tenth-eleventh century, with the legend, 'The All the One.' The alchemists repeated again and again that the *opus* came out of one thing and returned again to the one, it is in a certain sense a circle, like the dragon that bites its tail. Therefore the work is often called *circulare*, that is, circle forming. Mercury stands at the beginning and at the end of the work. It is the *prima materia*, first matter, it is the 'head of the crow,' the black or *nigredo*, as dragon he swallows himself, as dragon he dies but rises again as *lapis*. He is the colour play of the peacock's tail and the separation into the four elements. He is the hermaphrodite of the Beginning Being, who walks separately in the classical brother-sister pair and unites in the *conjunctio*, in order to appear again at the end in the radiant form of the *lumen novum*, the new light, the *lapis*. Mercury is metal and yet fluid; matter and yet spirit; cold and yet fiery; poison and yet medicine; it is a symbol of the uniting of the pair of opposites."

All these ideas are the oldest common property of alchemy. Zosimos, one of the oldest authorities, reports that Ostanes who long preceded him, says: "Go to the Nile and there you will find a stone which has a spirit in it. Take it and split it, and reach your hand into its inner parts and draw out its heart; its soul is in its heart." A commentator says of this stone that it refers to the expelling of quicksilver.

When Nietzsche says, "In the stone an image sleeps for me," he says the same thing but in reversed order. In the time of Zosimos the world was filled with the projection of the soul secret which appeared as the secret of matter. But the estatic intuition of Nietzsche was able to tear the secret of the superman out of the stone where it had been sleeping, and was able to produce a picture of the divine man in accordance with this image, a symbol which was to him not the spirit of the stone, but a human ideal, the superman.

The old alchemists did the reverse. They sought the wonder stone which contained a spiritual being, in order to obtain that spirit stuff which inheres in all bodies, and can change all ignoble matter into noble, through colour changes.

This spiritual stuff is like quicksilver which inheres invisibly in ore (presumably they referred here to an ore containing small quantities of mercury) and must be extracted if one wants to obtain it *in substantia* (in its own substance). When one has it one can project it upon other imperfect bodies and lead them over into perfection. They say that the imperfect condition is like sleep, the imperfect bodies are like those chained and sleeping in Hades, who are awakened to a beautiful new life by the wonder stone.

Nietzsche took care that no one should mistake the superman for the spiritual or ideal moral man, and the alchemists also state that the tincture, or divine water, not only has a beneficent effect, but is also the most deadly poison.

This same Zosimos recommended that a certain woman who was in need of transformation should be baptised in the Crater. The Crater refers to the divine chalice of which Hermes spoke to Thoth. After the Creation God sent it to earth, filled with *Nous*, that is, spirit or consciousness, so that men might be baptised in it and free themselves from their sleeping condition and take part in the higher consciousness.

In these sayings of Zosimos we realize that he found his own unconscious mystic philosophy projected into matter. In his experiments he must have experienced an identity between his own soul happening and the behaviour of the materials in his retort. But this was naturally unknown to Zosimos, who merely encountered the process in matter. The uncon-

[ 12 ]

scious content betrayed itself, as it always does, in dreams, visions, phantasies, and so forth. For the unconscious content is an autonomous complex and leads a self-sufficient existence in the psychological non-ego, where it is unconscious; but when it is constellated or attracted by outer analogies, it immediately projects itself.

There are many forms of the vision of the *Nous*, the spirit, coming to earth. The Neo-Pythogoreans said that the soul was swallowed by man as far as the *Nous*, which however remained outside of man, as his daemon. The Gnostics have a legend of how the *Nous* bent down to earth and saw his image in matter, Physis, and fell in love with his own image and Physis, physical nature, embraced him and they gave birth to seven hermaphroditic beings. And then there is the Christian formulation at the beginning of the Gospel of John, where it is related that the Light fell into the darkness of matter, when Mary, that is the earth, conceived the Son of God, and later that he released himself from matter in order to save all souls. This corresponds to the unconscious content projected into matter and rescued again from the projection through the alchemical work.

In such vision reflections, Jung tells us, the projection of an autonomous content comes to expression. They correspond to dreams and phantasies. In the examples he gave, only some of which I have repeated, the projected content is the *Nous*, or understanding, the Anthropos or God-man, and the *pneuma*, or spirit. As analytical psychology, Jung continues, is based on the assumption that psychic contents are realities, we must regard the qualities projected as corresponding to a real though unconscious part of the personality. In the instances given this unconscious part must possess a higher consciousness than the ego personality, corresponding to the projected contents, which are superior to the average man. Actually such figures as the *Nous* or the Anthropos always express superior insights or qualities which are still not conscious, and about which it is doubtful whether they can be attributed to the ego or not. This is a very important point. For if the ego becomes identified to these figures a disastrous inflation will inevitably occur. And Jung utters a very serious warning against such an identification.

The qualities projected, in the examples he cites, have rarely, until quite recent times, been attributed to the human personality. The one great exception is Christ. He was God and Man, the manifestation of the divine *Nous*. This is the Christian projection; the pagan (alchemical) passes beyond man and meets the unknown in the world of matter, that unknown substance which is in some way filled with God. As in Christianity, the

[ 13 ]

Godhead conceals Himself in the unknown and despised man, so in alchemical philosophy He conceals Himself in the unprepossessing stone. The spirit descends into the inferior parts of dead matter which is of feminine nature and ruled over by evil; it is the *anima mundi*, the soul of the world, the Physis who longs for the embrace of *Nous*, the spirit.

These myth pictures, says Jung, paint a drama of the human soul played behind and beyond our human consciousness. In it man is both the one to be redeemed and the Redeemer. The first is the Christian formulation; the second the alchemistic. In the first, man takes to himself the need to be redeemed and abandons the accomplishment of the redemption, the true *opus*, to the autonomous divine figure. In the second, man takes upon himself the duty for the performance of the redeeming work, while he ascribes the suffering condition to matter, which is therefore the one in need of redemption. In both cases the work of redemption is an *opus*.

In Christianity the reconciliation with God is brought about by the life and death of the divine man, who was both God or Spirit, and man or body. The human man as bearer of a soul sunk in the world, that is, the flesh, was placed through a synchronistic happening in relation to God at the moment when God, the Spirit, descended into earth in the incarnation as the Son of Mary, who is the *Virgo Terra*, Virgin Earth. And man was potentially redeemed when He returned to the Father. Through Christ's sacrifice of Himself man is redeemed. This sacrifice the Church repeated and brought to completion in the Mass, the *Officium* or *Opus Divinum*. The sacrifice of the Mass is far more than an *oblation*, an offering of bread and wine. The transformation of the elements makes it a real sacrifice of the body of Christ. In the ritual of the Greek Church this is clearly shown. There before the consecration the priest cuts a slice from the loaf of bread saying, "As a lamb He is led to the slaughter." Then he lays the slice on the altar, saying, "Sacrificed is the Lamb of God." Then he imprints a sign of the cross on the bread and stabs it in the side with a little lance saying, "And one of the soldiers pierced His side with a lance and blood and water flowed out." With these words water and wine are mixed in the cup.

In the Roman as well as in the Greek ritual the priest recounts the traditional events and thus Christ in the sacramental condition possesses a *vita corporea actualis*, a true corporeal life. And so a physical death of His body takes place again. This is called the *mortificatio*. [I would call your attention to the fact that this is one of the stages of the alchemical process, where after the *conjunctio*, the uniting of male and female, of soul and body, the king dies or is dissolved.]

Then in the Mass follows the consecration of the elements and the trans-substantiation of the bread and wine, by which they pass over out of the imperfect, marred condition into a subtle body. The bread signifies body, and the wine as blood the soul. After the transformation has taken place a small piece of the consecrated bread, the Host, is mixed with the wine, which represents the *conjunctio* of the soul of Christ with His body. After the transformation the bread was called *medicina*. It is the healing means or medicine of immortality, which extends its beneficent work to the communion of the believers, bringing about the uniting of soul and body, which in the words of the Mass, is a healing of the *soul* and a reformation of the body. In the prayers following Communion we read, "God who considered Himself to be worthy *(dignatus est)* to be a sharer of the humanity of man." Dr. Jung says that as a Protestant he marvelled at this and adds, "Surely man must also be worthy to be a sharer of God's divinity."

The action of the priest causes the transformation; it is he who redeems the creatures of bread and wine from their imperfection. Here he is himself a redeemer and the problem of redemption is turned around. Not man but matter, in which the divine soul is hid in a sleeping chained condition, is the one in need of redemption. But matter in which lies this divine secret is also in the human body; it is cheap and is found everywhere, even in filth. Therefore the great work is no longer a ritual *officium*, but the work of redemption accomplished by God himself through Christ in humanity, which was a pattern, but which now the alchemist, the philosopher, must recognize as his individual work, if he has received the *donum spiritus sancti*, which is the divine art. But this work has to be done each for himself. The alchemists stress this point, saying that the results you obtain will be far from the truth if you work through another, either a servant or a master, "whoever works as a laboratory assistant will never be received into the presence of the Queen." We can see here a striking similarity to our experience in analysis, where no amount of familiarity with analytic ideals serves to transform the personality. Only the direct experience of the unconscious in the actual performing of the work, the *opus*, can effect a transformation.

So we see that the alchemical work was a process intended to redeem the divine spark from matter where it lies hidden. One of the alchemical legends relates how the King's son lies buried in the depths of the sea. He seems lifeless, but really lives and calls out for help. Few pay attention to his lament; they do not seem to be concerned with the treasure he promises nor with the healing. Jung says of this parable: The King is lifeless, that is in a condition of latency; he is in the depths of the sea, which means that the content, being unconscious, is projected. But this content belongs to the personality if it is to be whole; there is therefore a fascination about it, the cry. Consciousness should do something about this cry, one should render service to the king. But this requires a descent into the darkness of the unconscious, the adventure of the night journey, in order to overcome death and restore life.

In the vision of Arisleus, recounted in the *Rosarium Philosophorum*, of 1550, this same theme is taken up but is told in much greater detail. In his vision Arisleus tells about his adventure with Rex Marinus, in whose kingdom nothing flourished and nothing propagated for there were no philosophers there and they alone have the secret of mixing things that are unlike. So the philosopher advised the king to mate his two children, Thabritius and Beya, who had been born in his brain. The brother and sister were brought before the philosopher and mated. Immediately the brother died and his body dissolved and disappeared. This is the death penalty following the incestuous *conjunctio oppositorum*, or union of the opposites, male and female, spirit and body. The youth is spirit, his sister body. The youth disappears entirely, either into the womb of Beya in coitus or, according to another version, the father swallows him. This is the complete descent of spirit into matter. In the vision the philosopher found himself in the greatest danger because of this death. Consciousness seems to have quenched itself in the unconscious. The hero is eaten by the dragon. When this happens, as in the similar experiences of analysis, it causes the utmost terror, which is the ghost-fear, and is due to the breaking of a taboo which always carries the heaviest penalties.

Arisleus and his companion were then locked in a triple glass house with the body of Thabritius in order to bring him to life again. Beya was locked in also. It was very hot in the glass house, the equivalent of the descent into Hades, the burning heat of the night journey or the belly of the dragon. The philosophers gave themselves up freely to death in order to create a fruitful life in that region of the soul which formerly lay in unconsciousness and in the shadow of death. This great heat recalls the story of Shadrach, Meshach, and Abednego cast into the fiery furnace by King Nebuchadnezzar, and you will remember that when he went to see whether they were yet dead he had a vision of a fourth who had joined them who was "like to the Son of God." In his danger and distress Arisleus called upon his almost divine master, Pythagoras, and he sent his assistant,

Harphoretus, the originator of nourishment, to help them. With this the work was completed and Thabritius came to life again, which can mean only that Harphoretus had brought the food of immortality to restore Thabritius to life. While they lay in the glass house, Arisleus being completely passive, the tree which bears the food of life grew up. The determining action came not from Arisleus but from the master who sent his messenger to help him and indeed the alchemists reiterate that the secret knowledge can be received only as the gift of God or from the lips of a master. So here the life-giving food, the elixir, comes from the divine Pythagoras.

The cry for help of Arisleus has its parallel in the Mass in the prayer of intercession for the living and the dead which immediately precedes the consecration. In the vision, the fruits of the tree of immortality bring healing; in the Mass, the consecrated bread and wine also bring healing for the soul and reformation of the body, but in as much as moral and other effects are meant by the fruits of the Mass, it is rather different. For here the spirit of Christianity and of alchemy separate. Christ received the benefits of the Mass for Himself personally (He rose again and ascended into heaven), while the alchemist receives the fruits of immortality not primarily for himself but for the King's son who was brought to life by the *opus*. His aim is the completion of the sought-for substance, the *lapis* or the gold. To him it is more important to bring the substance to completion than himself.

The alchemist does not assume the rôle of redeemer through religious megalomania, indeed he assumes it far less than the priest. He always stresses his own humility, and does not identify himself with Christ; on the contrary, later alchemy identified the sought-for substance, the *lapis*, with Christ.

The earliest reference in which the stone is equated to the *Christus* idea, which Dr. Jung could find, was in the work of Raymond Lully, 1225-1313. The *Tractas Aureus* refers to the "stone rejected" in a way that suggests an analogy with Christ, but the *Margerita Pretiosa, The Pearl of Great Price*, of Petrus Bonus, dated 1330, is the first text to give this idea in detail. Here it is said that the art consists of two parts. The first, the natural part, takes one up to the sublimation, where through the mediation of the spirit, a radiating white stone is germinated and flies to heaven. This is the bright and manifest stone. This first part of the work must be followed by the second, or supernatural, part, in which the stone is fixed and made permanent. This effect is only brought about by divine aid through the addition of the secret stone which is not comprehended by the senses but only through inspiration or divine revelation, or through the teaching of a wise man. This secret stone is the gift of God; without it alchemy could not exist. In this part of the work God alone is the operator, while nature remains passive. This, you see, corresponds to the vision of Arisleus where in the glass house, that is, in the retort, Arisleus the natural man could only wait for the help of the perfected man, Pythagoras. "The stone," continues the text of *The Pearl of Great Price*, "after the disintegration is resurrected by the gift of God and becomes incorruptible and of unbelievable subtlety and able to penetrate everything solid. So the ancients knew that a virgin must conceive and bear, because in their art a stone conceives and becomes pregnant by itself and brings forth. Then God becomes man, and the creator and the created—the man and the boy—become one. Now because no creature with the exception of man can be united with God because of their dissimilarity, God must become one with man. And that happened with Jesus Christ and His Virgin Mother."

Thus in the beginning of the fourteenth century the relation between the mystery of Christ and that of the stone was recognized and the philosophical *opus* appeared as a parallel and a continuation of the divine work of redemption.

It would be expected that these two approaches, that of alchemy and of the church, would have produced a conflict for the man of the Middle Ages but there is little evidence of such a conflict. In the fifteenth or sixteenth century Nicholas Melchior even represented the alchemical *opus* under the form of the Mass.

In his private Mass service, Melchior inserts an *Ave Praeclara*, "Hail to the Radiant One," after the Gospel. This he named " 'Testament of the Art,' because the entire alchemical art is hidden in it." This Ave recounts how "the radiant light of the world unites with the moon, and becomes the tie of Mars and the *conjunctio* of Mercury." From these three the strong giant is born and they dissolve into the mercurial waters, the sperma of the philosophers. "The strong giant seeks to be united to the Virgin who becomes pregnant and so there arises the fortune-bringing embryo. Then there appears at the bottom of the chalice the strong Ethiopian, dead and lifeless. He begs to be buried and moistened and then by a miracle he is restored and is called Natural Sulphur, and their son is Lapis Philosophorum."

The order of the acts in Melchior's private Mass differs from the Church

[ 18 ]

ritual and may be an evidence of an intellectual conflict between the experience of the rite which has an external efficacy and the individual experience.

A further testimony of the lapis-Christus identification is to be found in the writings of George Ripley, Canon of Bridlington, who tells of the sterile king who ought to live under the wings of the sun. In order to be cured of his infirmity he needs to be born again. "He now wished to return again into the body of his mother and be dissolved in the *prima materia*. The mother stimulated him to this purpose and shortly concealed him under her garment until she had incarnated him again, through herself and in herself." He was born like the moon and shortly passed over into the brilliance of the sun. He had the weapons of the four elements and became a supreme conqueror, and healer of all diseases, and Redeemer of all sins. In the lap of the mother (now the Redeemed Virgin) lay the Green Lion from whose side blood flowed. She was crowned with a diadem and became a constellation in heaven.

This difficult vision Jung interprets as follows: The king is a man who suffers from spiritual barrenness because the projection of the unconscious cannot be developed any further until it is integrated with consciousness. The apotheosis of the Virgin, at the end, refers to the union of the soul and body of Mary after her death and her elevation to heaven, where she was enthroned Queen of Heaven, being the one in whom the material of the earth is transfigured as the ascending earthly *body* in which the God-head is taken up. This is in contrast to Christ who ascended in a resurrection body.

It becomes completely clear from this material, writes Jung, what it was that alchemy fundamentally sought. It desired to produce a subtle body, the transfigured resurrection body, corresponding to the Diamond Body, which Chinese alchemy sought to produce. So Orthelius, writing in the seventeenth century says, "The philosophers found no better means of healing than that which on account of its hardness, transparency, and ruby colour, they called the Stone of the Philosophers."

This same Orthelius in speaking of the *Word* distinguishes between the *Verbum Scriptum* and the *Verbum Factum*. In the first, he says Christ is in His swaddling clothes; in the latter the Word has became real in the creations of God, where we can touch it, as it were, with our hands. Out of this we must raise our treasure, for the Word is the fire, the life, the real Spirit. He continues, "This spirit is the *spiritus mundi* which brooded of old on the face of the waters, and now is the philosopher's stone, the real means through which body and soul are held together during our lifetime."

To him the divine medicine has become merely a means of holding body and soul together: The philosopher, who in earlier days, descended even into the darkness of Hades, in order to accomplish the work, has become in the seventeenth century a speculative worker only.

This change in alchemy was due principally to the work of Paracelsus, who is the ancestor of modern medical thought. For Paracelsus and Böehme split alchemy into two parts, natural science and Protestant mysticism, so that the stone of the philosophers is once again what it was aforetime—cheap of the cheapest, thrown out on the streets.

### EPILOGUE

One has to remember, in considering alchemy, that this philosophy played an important rôle in the Middle Ages; it developed a highly extensive literature which had a far-reaching influence on the contemporary life of the spirit. The claim which alchemy itself makes in this direction is best demonstrated by the lapis-Christus parallel. If one goes into the psychology of alchemistic thought, one finds traces of the soul of man which, in contrast to the conscious, has changed hardly at all over a period of many centuries, and one finds that a two-thousand year old truth is still the truth of to-day, that it is still living and effective. In this central place are those fundamental soul-facts which have always remained the same and always will remain the same. Yesterday and to-day, when viewed from this angle, appear as episodes of a drama begun in the dim ages of the past, which extends throughout the centuries into a distant future. This drama is an *Aurora Consurgens,* The Becoming Conscious of Humanity.

The alchemical process of classical time was a chemical search with which unconscious psychological material became mixed through a process of projection. The psychological condition of the work was therefore stressed many times in the texts. The unconscious contents which were observed in the work were those which are adapted for projection into the unknown chemical matter, and because the nature of matter is purely impersonal and factual, projection of impersonal, or collective archetypes, took place. In those centuries the life of the spirit was collective, thus it was the picture of the spirit caught in the darkness of the world which was principally recognized in matter. The spirit caught in matter was in an unredeemed condition, that is, it was relatively unconscious and that was felt as painful. The psychological condition of an unconscious content is always characterized by a pair of opposites, such as being and non-being, so that the uniting of the pair of opposites played a determining rôle in the alchemical process. Thus the outcome of the process carries the significance of the reconciling symbol, which naturally carries the projection of the Redeemer Image, hence the lapis-Christus parallel, and also the parallel between the redeeming work of the Mass, the *Officium Divinum*, and the chemical *magisterium*. The principal difference is that the Christian work is a work accomplished, the need of the redemption of man for the honour of God as Redeemer, while the alchemistic work is man's responsibility who as redeemer must help the waiting divine world soul, which sleeps in matter. In the Church formulation the work is done for mankind collectively; in the alchemistic work the individual man must find a means not only for his own salvation but also, which is more important, for the world spirit hidden in matter. These two standpoints are fundamentally opposed. The question is concerned with the pair of opposites "collective and individual," or "society and the individual." This is so modern a problem that it has required the exaggerated heaping up of the masses of our day to make the individual conscious at all of his suffocation in the fabric of the organized masses. In the Middle Ages the collectivism of the Church seldom exerted sufficient pressure on the individual to make the problem of his relation to society a general one. Therefore this problem remained at the level of projection and it was reserved to our time to approach at least an embryonic consciousness of it, under the mask of a neurotic individualism. Before this most recent change occurred, however, alchemy reached its climax in Goethe's *Faust*, which is interpenetrated from beginning to end with alchemistic ideas. What happens in *Faust* is most clearly expressed in the Paris-Helen scene. (In this scene Faust raised the spirits of Paris and Helen and then watched them move and act of themselves on a stage. This is of course an analogy to the phantasies we ourselves experience through active imagination. When, in the phantasy, Paris attempted to carry out the historical Rape of Helen, Faust interfered and himself approached Helen, turning his magic wand against Paris, who burst into flames. The vision vanished and Faust was stricken down unconscious.) For the alchemist of the Middle Ages this scene would signify the secret *conjunctio* of Sol and Luna in the retort; the modern man, however, clothed in the figure of Faust recognized that it was projection and placed himself in the position of Paris, or Sol, and took possession of Helen, or Luna, his feminine counterpart. Here appears the deeper reason why in this drama all attempts to produce the Holy Embryo, or Diamond Body, go up in fire and disappear. For Faust by identifying himself with Paris draws the alchemistic *conjunctio* out of the projection into the sphere of the personal-psychological experience and thus into consciousness. This critical step signifies nothing less than the solution of the alchemistic riddle and the redemption of a part of the personality, which has been unconscious up to this time. But every increase in consciousness carries with it the danger of inflation, which is clearly depicted in Faust's superhuman powers. His death was a historical necessity, but not a satisfactory answer. The birth and transformation, Euphorion, child of Helen and Faust, which followed upon the *conjunctio*, passed over into the beyond, that is, into the unconscious, but there remained unsolved the problem of the transformation of the individual into the superman, which Nietzsche took up in *Zarathustra*. Nietzsche, however, brought the superman into the most dangerous proximity to the conscious ego-personality, and so unavoidably called forth Christian resentment against the idea, for his superman is a hybris of individual consciousness which was aimed directly against the collective power of Christendom, and could only lead to a catastrophic disturbance of the individual consciousness. It is well known how and in what an exceedingly striking form the alchemical *"tam ethice quam physice"* happened to Nietzsche in his actual insanity, and how the subsequent years produced a collective superman corresponding to the individualism of the Nietzschean superman: the totalitarian state, which mocked at all former achievement. Suffocation of the individual on the one hand, Christendom sickening, possibly wounded to death, on the other, that is the stark antithesis of our time.

Faust's sin was identification with the transforming and the transformed. Nietzsche's arrogance was identification with the superman, Zarathustra, that part of the personality which was reaching up into consciousness. But can one rightly speak of Zarathustra as a part of the personality? Is he not rather the superhuman factor in which man indeed has a part, but which he is not? When Nietzsche explains God as missing is He really dead? Has He not withdrawn into the disguise of the superman?

To return to Faust, at the end of the drama, urged on by the blind pressure of the superman, he caused the death of Philemon and Baucis. But who are these two modest old people? When the world had become godless and there was no hospitable resting-place for the divine strangers, Jupiter and Mercury, Philemon and Baucis alone welcomed the superhuman guests and when Baucis wanted to sacrifice her last goose for them the transformation occurred; the gods became manifest; the modest hut became a temple, and the old people the servants of the sanctuary. And these are the ones whom Faust could not tolerate.

In a certain sense the old alchemists stand nearer to the soul-truth than Faust, for they sought to redeem the fiery spirit from the chemical elements, and they treated the *mysterium* as if it lay in the dark and silent lap of nature. It was still outside themselves; they did not identify with the projection. The upward pressing development of consciousness has first to resolve this projection and restore to the soul what was from the beginning a part of the soul's nature. But, one asks, what had the soul become since the days of enlightenment and scientific rationalism? It had become identical with consciousness. Soul became that which I know and was in no way outside of the ego. For this reason it was unavoidable that identification should take place with the contents withdrawn from the projection. This caused an inflation of consciousness which could only be quenched by the most frightful catastrophe to culture, represented in *Faust* by the deluge which the Gods sent to inhospitable humanity, after the death of Philemon and Baucis.

An inflated consciousness is always egocentric and conscious only of its own present. It is incapable of learning from the past, incapable of grasping the present; and incapable of drawing right conclusions in regard to the future. It is hypnotised by itself and therefore does not permit itself to talk with itself. It is therefore doomed to catastrophes which necessarily strike it dead. Inflation is in a paradoxical sense a becoming unconscious of consciousness. This is the situation which comes to pass when consciousness takes to itself the contents of the unconscious and loses the capacity to differentiate, for differentiation is the *sine qua non* of all consciousness.

When Europe's fate dramatized a war of grandiose horror, a war which no one wanted, for which no one had, so to speak, asked—who then really caused this war and its continuation? No one noted the fact that the European was possessed by something which robbed him of all free self-determination. This possessed and unconscious condition will continue up to the point where the European becomes for the first time afraid of his god-almightiness. But this is a change which can only begin with individuals, for masses as everyone knows well enough are blind animals. Therefore it seems to me, says Jung, of some importance when at least individuals begin to understand that there are psychological contents which do not belong to the ego personality, but are to be ascribed far more to a psychical non-ego. This recognition must always be made fully con-

[ 23 ]

scious if one wishes to avoid a threatening inflation. To help us to this there are the useful and edifying archetypes which poets and philosophers point out to us, and which may well be designated as healing means for men and times. Of course this is not anything that one can hold up to the masses, but always something hidden which one can place before himself in the stillness. But few wish to know anything about it, for it is so much easier to proclaim the panacea for the ten thousand others which one need then no longer apply to himself; for every suffering has an end, we all know, if only very many are in agreement. In the herd there are no doubts, and the greater multitude always has the better truth—but also the greater catastrophes.

What we can learn from our prototypes is first of all the fact that the soul contains contents or exists under influences, whose assimilation is associated with the greatest dangers. When the old alchemists ascribed their secret to matter, and when neither Faust nor Zarathustra stirred us to want to incorporate this content in our ego, nothing remained but to reject the arrogant claim of consciousness to be the soul itself and to recognize a reality of the soul, which we with our present means of understanding are nevertheless unable to comprehend. The man who accepts his not knowing is no ignoramus, says Jung, but not so the man whose consciousness has not yet reached the point in its development where he knows about his not knowing. The alchemistic expectation of being able to produce philosophical gold from matter, or to make the panacea or the wonder stone was, Jung concludes, an illusion caused by projection, but it corresponded to psychological facts which have a great significance in the psychology of the unconscious.

The alchemist, as the texts and their symbols show, projected the so-called individuation process into chemical transformations. But the scientific term individuation does not mean at all that it concerns an unquestionably known and clarified fact. It only designates the still unexplored and very dark territory of the personality-mirroring processes of the unconscious. It concerns the processes of life, which lie behind phenomena and are sensed but never known, and have for this reason from the very beginning of things given the most significant impulse towards symbol formation. These processes are secret insofar as they present riddles to the human understanding, about whose solution it has been concerned for a long time, and perhaps in vain. It is indeed doubtful whether in the last analysis the understanding is a fitting instrument or not. Not in vain is alchemy spoken of as "art," with the correct feeling that it concerns form-processes which can be comprehended only in the experience, but spoken about only intellectually. Let us not forget, Jung concludes, that alchemy coined the dictum:

"*Rumpite libros, ne corda vestra rumpantur,*" tear up your books that your hearts be not torn into shreds.

CPSIA information can be obtained at www.ICGtesting.com
Printed in the USA
LVOW061921061112

306128LV00013B/15/P